Dor Dragon

Original story by Yvonne Cook
Illustrated by Helen Humphries and Phil Garner

It's raining.
Dom and his cat
are at home.

2

3

4

Dragons have got two eyes.

Blue eyes or green eyes?

Big eyes or small eyes?

Let me see!

10

Dom's dragon has got a white head, blue eyes, big, green teeth and a purple and green body.

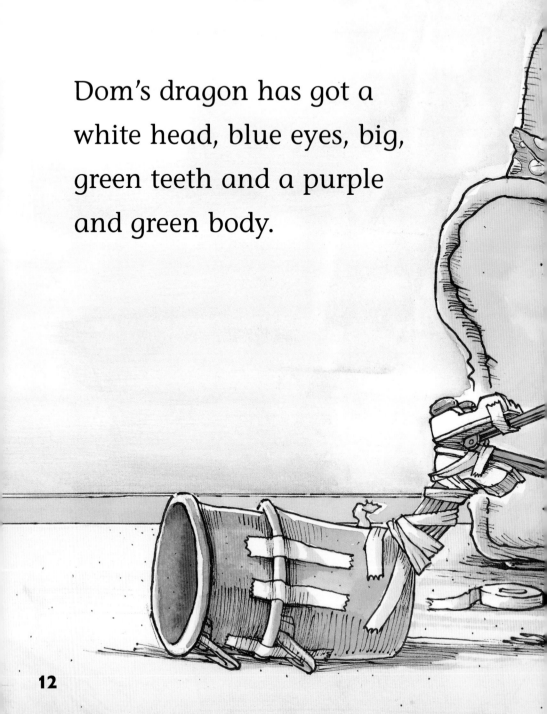

13

Dom, his cat and the dragon go for a walk in the rain.

Picture Dictionary

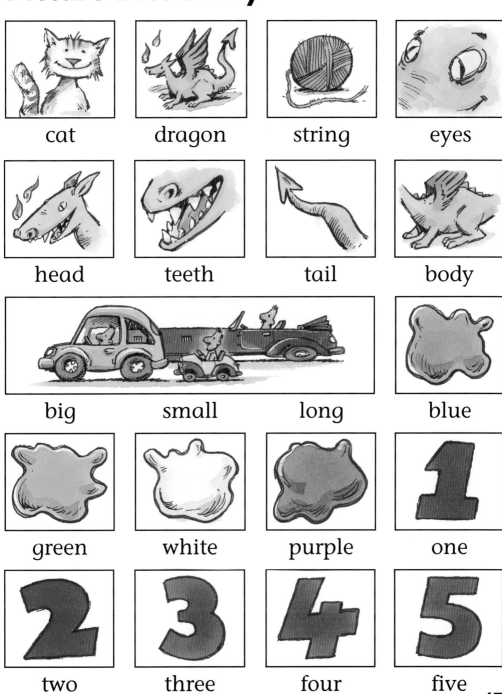

cat

dragon

string

eyes

head

teeth

tail

body

big

small

long

blue

green

white

purple

one

two

three

four

five

Activities

1 Colour the dragon.

teeth  head eyes body tail

18

2 Look at pages 4 and 5. (Circle) the number of dragons you can see.

3 Match the pictures and the numbers.

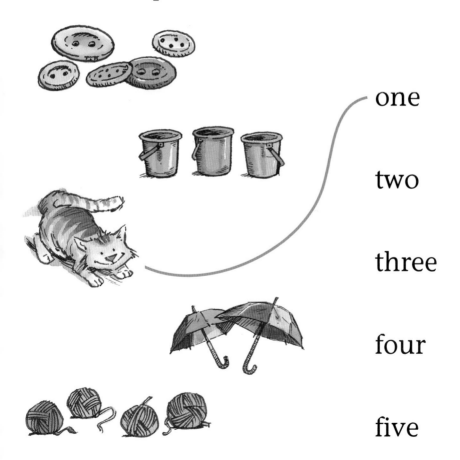

one

two

three

four

five

Macmillan Education
Between Towns Road, Oxford OX4 3PP
A division of Macmillan Publishers Limited
Companies and representatives throughout the world

ISBN 978 1 4050 2502 7
ISBN 978 1 4050 5718 9 (International Edition)

First published 2002 Macmillan Education Australia Pty Ltd
This edition © Macmillan Publishers Limited 2004

Illustrated by Helen Humphries and Phil Garner

Printed in China

2011 2010 2009
10 9 8 7 6   Spain
13 12 11 10   International